Elf Games

Page 1

Page 2

Page 3

Page 4

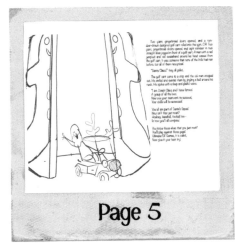

Page 5

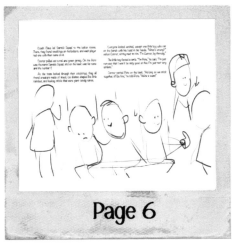

Page 6

Page 7

Page 8

Page 9

Page 10

Page 11 - 12

Page 13 - 14

Page 15

Page 16

Page 17

Page 18

A FAMILY PROJECT

Elf Games

GAME ON!

OUR FAMILY, OUR STORY, OUR BOOK

Dedicated to Addison, Brady, and Jordan.
Never lose your imagination.

The Elf Games
1 East Erie St
Suite 525 PMB 4295
Chicago, IL 60611
www.theelfgames.com

Ordering Information:
Quantity sales. Special discounts are available on quantity purchases by corporations, associations, and others. For details, contact The Elf Games at the address above.
Printed in China. First Edition

ISBN - 978-1-7342830-3-7

Elf Games

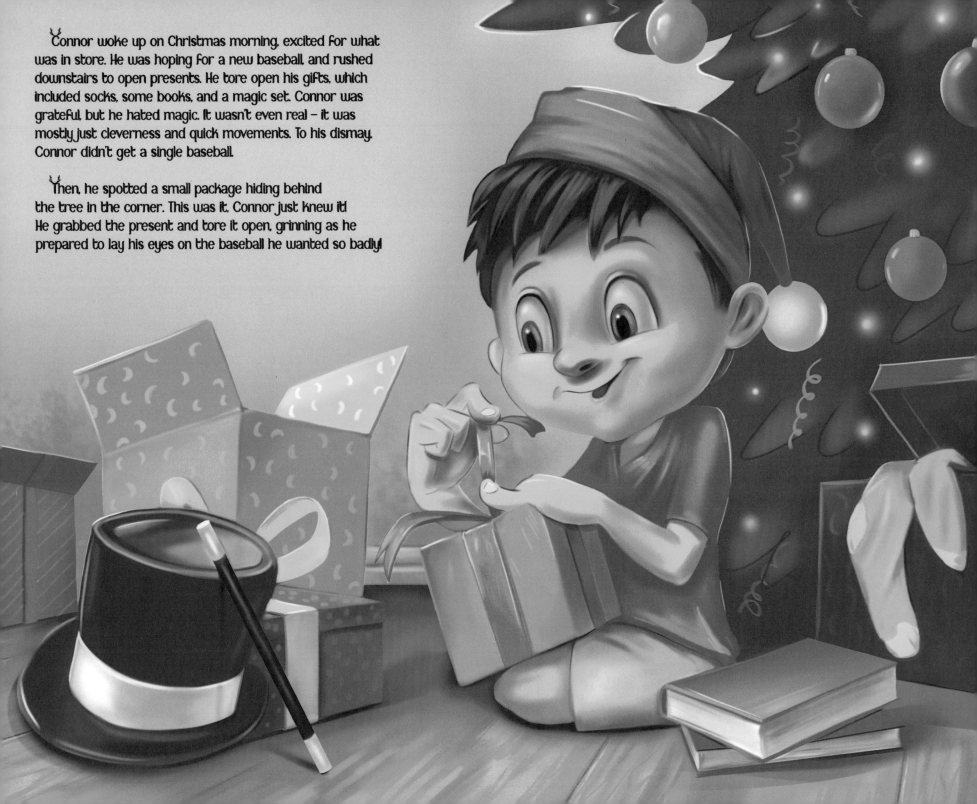

Connor woke up on Christmas morning, excited for what was in store. He was hoping for a new baseball, and rushed downstairs to open presents. He tore open his gifts, which included socks, some books, and a magic set. Connor was grateful, but he hated magic. It wasn't even real – it was mostly just cleverness and quick movements. To his dismay, Connor didn't get a single baseball.

Then, he spotted a small package hiding behind the tree in the corner. This was it, Connor just knew it! He grabbed the present and tore it open, grinning as he prepared to lay his eyes on the baseball he wanted so badly!

As the official Santa Claus,
I would like to enlist
All the girls and all the boys
Who are on the Nice List.

Because you made the Nice List, friend,
You have a chance to play
In some exciting yuletide games,
Right after Christmas Day.

Tomorrow morning when you wake
Just spin this small globe thrice,
And say these magic words to reach
The land of snow and ice:

"It's time to join the greatest team!
It's time to score a goal!
It's time to leave my home for now!
And go to the North Pole!"

Instead of a baseball, though, Connor was looking at...
well, he didn't know what he was looking at. It was a white orb,
a smooth globe with nothing but a tiny, red-and-white striped
pole at the top. Connor shrugged and pulled on the little pole,
revealing a small compartment with a rolled-up piece of paper
inside.

Connor unrolled the tiny scroll and read the words written
with fancy letters.

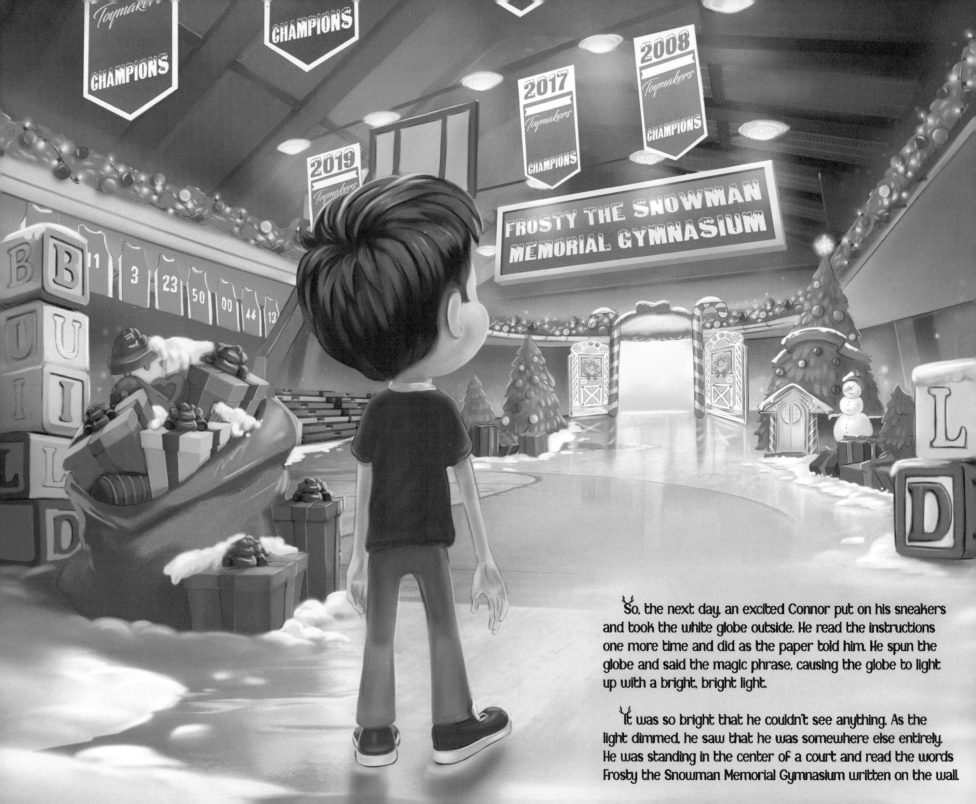

So, the next day, an excited Connor put on his sneakers and took the white globe outside. He read the instructions one more time and did as the paper told him. He spun the globe and said the magic phrase, causing the globe to light up with a bright, bright light.

It was so bright that he couldn't see anything. As the light dimmed, he saw that he was somewhere else entirely. He was standing in the center of a court and read the words Frosty the Snowman Memorial Gymnasium written on the wall.

Soon, there were more flashes of light and nine other kids appeared in the gymnasium! They all looked around and started chatting excitedly. After a few minutes, they heard small footsteps and saw ten elves running towards them.

One of the elves jumped up on Connor's shoulder and spoke in a high voice.

"My name is Chocolate Chip Cookie,
But you can call me Chip.
Stand still so I can measure you,
I'll make it really quick!

Why are we doing this, you ask?
Now please, let me inform,
We need to get your sizes for
A brand-new uniform!"

Two giant, gingerbread doors opened, and a
reindeer designed golf cart rolled into the gym.
A man with a red jumpsuit and red sweatband
around his head waved from the golf cart.
It was someone that none of the kids had met
before, but all of them recognized.

"Santa Claus!" they all yelled.

The golf cart came to a stop and the old man stepped
out. He smiled and quieted them by jingling a bell around
his neck. He spoke with a deep and gleeful voice.

"I am Coach Claus and I have formed
A group of all the best.
Now use your teamwork to succeed,
Your skills will be assessed!

You all are part of Santa's Squad
Now isn't that just neat?
Hockey, baseball, football too –
Is how you'll all compete!

You know those elves that you just met?
You'll play against those guys!
The Elf Games, it is called,
Now give it your best try!

Coach Claus led Santa's Squad to the locker rooms. There, they found stockings on the lockers, and each player had one with their name on it.

Connor pulled out a red and green jersey. On the front was the name Santa's Squad, and on the back was his name and the number 1!

As the team looked through their stockings, they all found sneakers made of tinsel, ice skates shaped like little reindeer, and hockey sticks that were giant candy canes.

Everyone looked excited, except one little boy who sat on the bench with his head in his hands. "What's wrong?" asked Connor, sitting next to him. "I'm Connor, by the way."

The little boy forced a smile. "I'm Pete," he said. "I'm just nervous that I won't be very good at this. I'm just not very athletic."

Connor patted Pete on the back. "As long as we stick together, it'll be fine," he told Pete. "We're a team!"

Connor and the rest of Santa's Squad made their way to the frozen lake, which was right beside a grove of gumdrop trees. The elves, also known as Team Toymakers, were already there lacing up their skates.

Coach Claus skated up and jingled his bell as Santa's Squad was stuffing their shoulders with teddy bears. He handed them a list of the rules and then started his pep talk.

You are here 'cause you're good, now it's time to be great!
So, grab onto those sticks, and lace up those skates!
It is time to play hockey – the first of our games,
I'll start out by calling each player by name!

On Darryl, on Dani, on Pete, Jan, and Vicky,
On Connor, on Rhonda, on Don, Liz and Ricky,
Keep your eye on the puck, keep your eye on the ball,
Now skate and play, run and play, pass and play, all!

"Coach Claus," said Connor. "The rules say magic is allowed, but we don't know any magic!"

The jolly old coach didn't hear him, though, over the sound of the cheering crowd.

The referee, a carrot-nosed snowman, placed the puck, a delicious smelling Christmas cookie, on the ice. He jingled a bell and the match began!

Connor raced towards the puck and swung, but he realized the candy cane was shorter than he thought. All the hockey sticks were elf-sized! He had to bend a little lower, but it was too late! Chip took control of the puck and sped past Connor.

"Block him!" Connor yelled at Vicky, the goalie. She bent forward to block the puck from entering the net made of Christmas lights, but the scent from the cookie-puck entered her nose. She closed her eyes delightedly... allowing the puck to soar right past.

One point for Team Toymakers. The elves cheered.

It was Santa's Squad's turn with the puck. Don, one of their best hockey players, maneuvered the puck down the rink and raised his stick. As he swung, though, his candy cane shattered against the ice.

"What on Earth?" Connor looked at the elves, who were sprinkling magic dust from their fingers on the candy canes. That must have been how they kept their hockey sticks from breaking. Coach Claus was on the sidelines with his hands on his head. Two reindeer provided commentary from their booth made of blocks.

"Now Dasher, it's not looking good for the Squad,
How they even got here, to me, is just odd."

"You're right, Blitzen, not sure if they can come back,
They'll have to improve on their plan of attack!"

www.theelfgames.com

Coach Claus jingled his bell and called a timeout. As they huddled, Connor had an idea. He pulled some stuffing out of the teddy bear in his shoulders and put it in Vicky's nose. He skated up to a gumdrop tree and pulled off the stickiest piece of candy he could find. He spread it all over his candy-cane-hockey-stick, and his teammates did the same.

"Isn't this cheating?" asked Pete.

Connor shook his head. "The rules say, 'Magic is allowed.' The elves are using magic to keep their candy canes from breaking – this is just our magic – cleverness and quick thinking!"

This time, things were different. Vicky wasn't distracted by the delicious scent because of the stuffing in her nostrils. She stopped the puck every time it came her way!

The hockey sticks stayed together because of the sticky gumdrops! The candy canes didn't shatter for the rest of the game, and even Pete made a few goals!

When time was up, the snowman referee jingled the bell. The score was 3 to 1, with Santa's Squad coming through victorious. They had won!

Santa's Squad cheered, but the games were not over. Next, they made their way to the baseball diamond, with an outfield covered in snow outside a dusty, brown infield. There was even a chocolate fountain past the outfield fence.

The crowd cheered for the elves as they made their way to the dugout.

Take me out of the workshop,
Take me out from the toys.
Buy me some cookies and Christmas snacks.
I don't care if we never go back.

For it's root, root, root for Toy Makers
If they don't win, they get coal.
For it's one, two, three strikes
you're naughty at the old North Pole!"

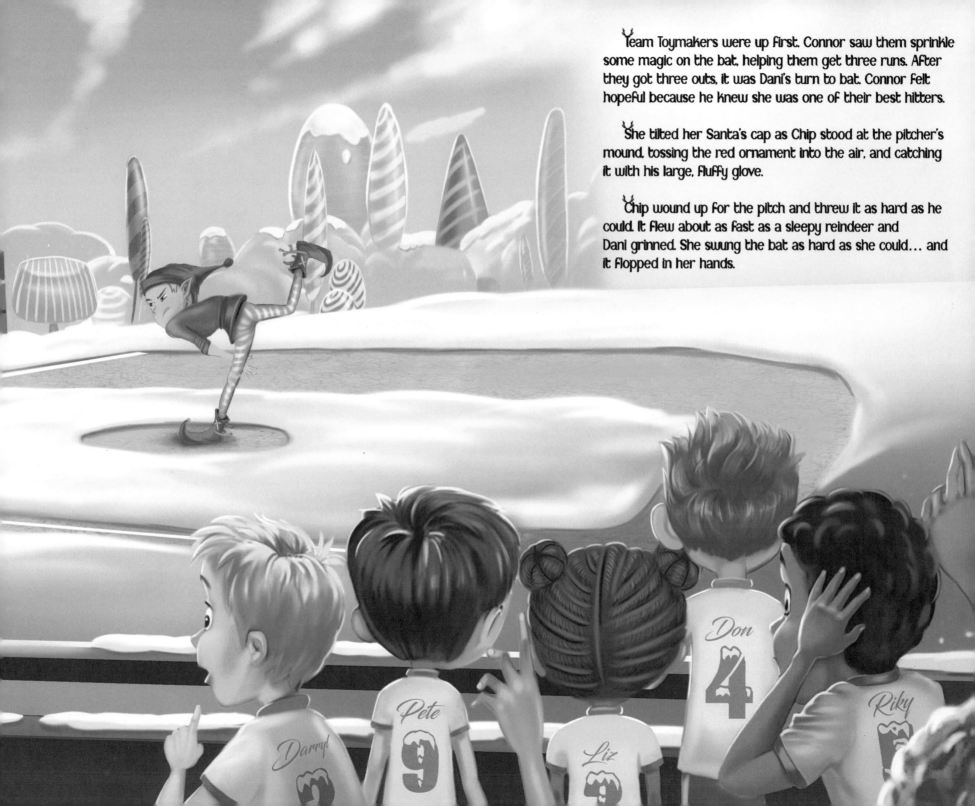

Team Toymakers were up first. Connor saw them sprinkle some magic on the bat, helping them get three runs. After they got three outs, it was Dani's turn to bat. Connor felt hopeful because he knew she was one of their best hitters.

She tilted her Santa's cap as Chip stood at the pitcher's mound, tossing the red ornament into the air, and catching it with his large, fluffy glove.

Chip wound up for the pitch and threw it as hard as he could. It flew about as fast as a sleepy reindeer and Dani grinned. She swung the bat as hard as she could… and it flopped in her hands.

"That swing you made, it is strike one,
But maybe next you'll get a run!"
called the gingerbread umpire.

Dani frowned, then straightened the bat, getting ready
to swing once again. Chip pitched the ornament and Dani
swung. Like last time, the bat flopped in her hands just as
she was about to make contact with the ornament.

"You missed again, and that's strike two,
There's only one more shot for you!"
yelled the gingerbread umpire.

Dani huffed and stretched out the bat so far that Connor was worried it would snap in half. She stared intently at the ornament as Chip wound up and pitched one more time. Swinging the bat as hard as she could, however, only caused it to flop so much that it wrapped around her body.

"That's it! You're done! You've reached strike three! You're out, that's how it has to be!" Shouted the gingerbread umpire, to a loud applause from the elves in the crowd.

Coach Claus put his hand on his face and shook his head. Dani walked sadly over to the dugout and handed the bat to Ricky. It flopped in his hands. Ricky sniffed the bat, then took a bite.

"It's licorice!" he said with a grin, "And it's delicious."
"But we'll never win a game with a bat like that," said Pete, nearly in tears, "No matter how delicious it is."

"We still need to try," said Connor. "We can't give up!"

Still, Santa's Squad reached three outs without even getting a hit.

When it was Team Toymakers' turn to bat, they knocked it out of the park – literally. When bases were loaded, Chip swung his stick of licorice with elven magic and skill, causing the ornament to soar over all of Santa's Squad's heads. Darryl raced after the ornament, but it flew past the fence, landing with a splat in the chocolate fountain. It was a home run.

The crowd roared as the elves made their way around the bases.

Darryl reached into the fountain and fished out the ornament. He threw it to Connor, but the weight of the chocolate caused it to fall to the ground before it reached the pitcher's mound. Connor picked it up and saw that the snow from the ground had hardened the chocolate on the ornament.

"Guys, I have an idea," said Connor, once Team Toymakers had three outs, "It's time for some more kid magic…"

Connor had everyone in Santa's Squad get their licorice bats and dip them in the chocolate fountain. Once their bats were good and chocolatey, the team rolled them in the snow.

Up in the commentator's booth, two reindeer discussed what they were seeing:

"Dasher, I think this team here,
Has gone and lost their minds."

"I think that you're right, Blitzen,
Because they're so far behind."

Liz was up now. She held her bat and smiled. She wiggled it in her hand, and thanks to the chocolate hardened by the cold snow, it didn't flop one bit. Chip tossed the ornament and watched sadly as it made contact with the licorice–chocolate–snow–bat, and soared to left field.

As Santa's squad cheered, Liz made it safely to first base. They were back in the game!

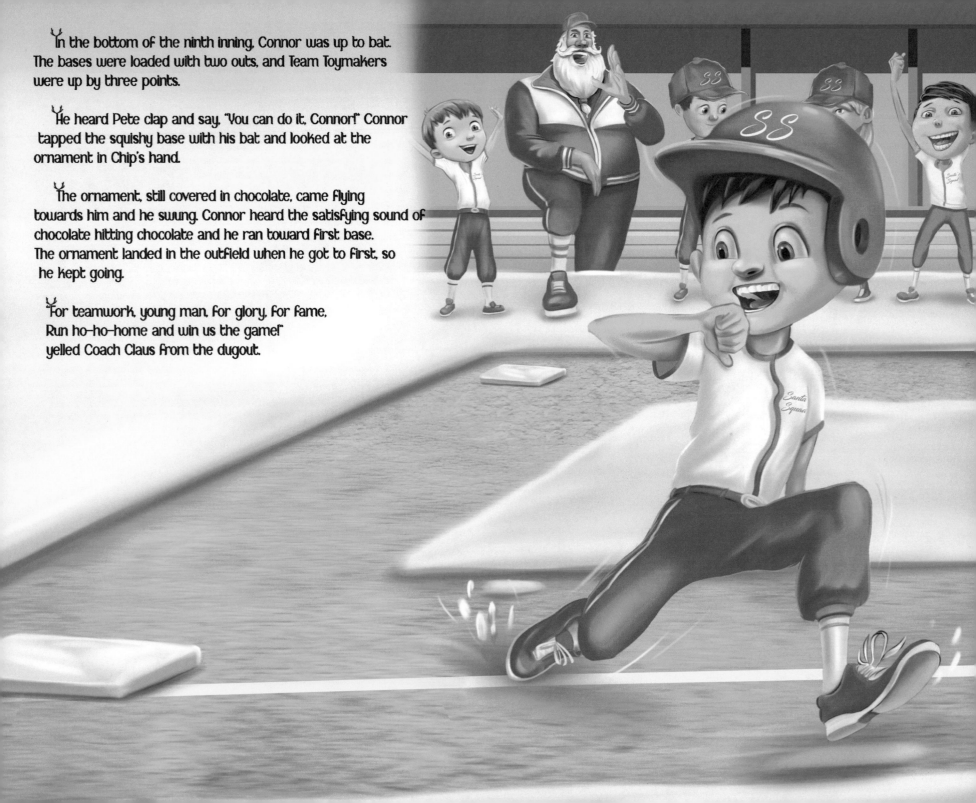

In the bottom of the ninth inning, Connor was up to bat. The bases were loaded with two outs, and Team Toymakers were up by three points.

He heard Pete clap and say, "You can do it, Connor!" Connor tapped the squishy base with his bat and looked at the ornament in Chip's hand.

The ornament, still covered in chocolate, came flying towards him and he swung. Connor heard the satisfying sound of chocolate hitting chocolate and he ran toward first base. The ornament landed in the outfield when he got to first, so he kept going.

"For teamwork, young man, for glory, for fame,
Run ho-ho-home and win us the game!"
yelled Coach Claus from the dugout.

Chip was standing right in his way. Connor would have to take drastic measures if he wanted to get to home plate.

The elf's legs were too short for Connor to get under, though. That meant only one thing – he would have to go over!

Connor leapt over Chip and dove headfirst for the ground. As he slid toward home, he tried to close his mouth... but he was too late. He got a mouthful of dirt.

Except... it wasn't dirt, it was cookie crumbs! He slid into home, his lips smacking into the soft base... a marshmallow!

The gingerbread umpire threw his arms into the air.

"Ran, ran, ran, as fast as he did,
This player's safe, you've won the game kid!"

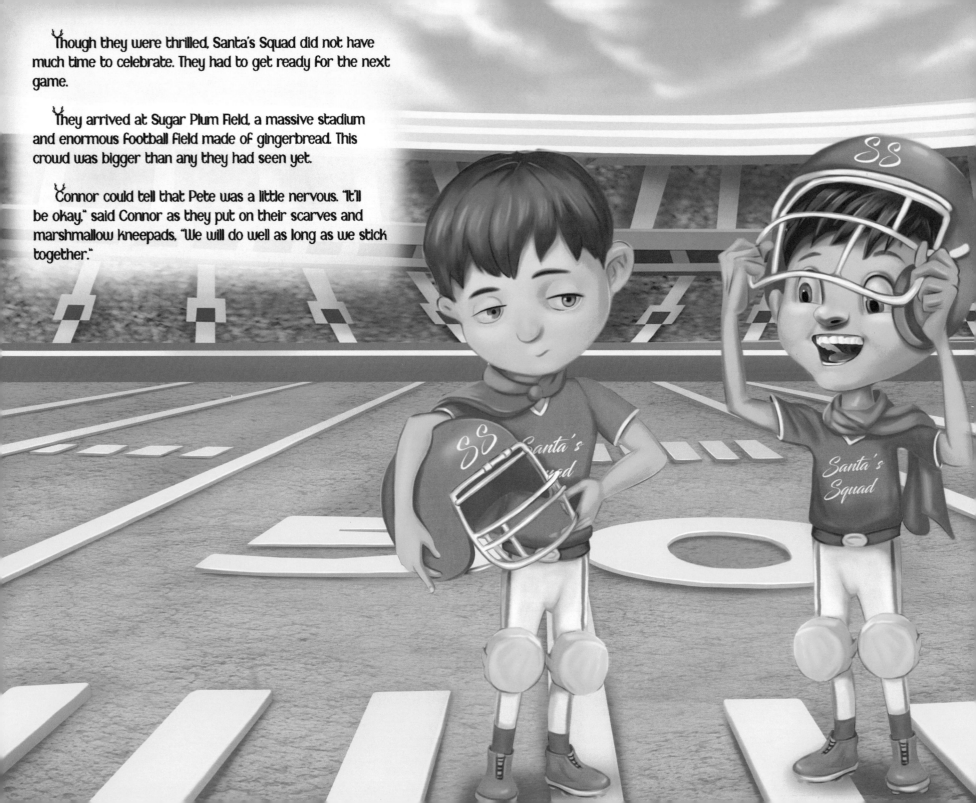

Though they were thrilled, Santa's Squad did not have much time to celebrate. They had to get ready for the next game.

They arrived at Sugar Plum Field, a massive stadium and enormous football field made of gingerbread. This crowd was bigger than any they had seen yet.

Connor could tell that Pete was a little nervous. "It'll be okay," said Connor as they put on their scarves and marshmallow kneepads, "We will do well as long as we stick together."

Pete smiled as the referee, a nutcracker, jingled a bell and called the teams to the field. He opened his mouth wide when he spoke.

"Players, be fair, and it will be a breeze.
Take someone's scarf, and no tackling, please.
Don't be a nut, or you will make me crack,
Now let's flip a coin, called by this quarterback!"

The nutcracker pointed at Jan, who called out heads. He flipped a gold coin and it landed on tails. Nodding at Team Toymakers, the nutcracker pulled a chestnut out of his mouth and tossed it to Chip.

"That's what you use for a football?" asked Connor.

Chip nodded with a smile, spinning the chestnut with a little magic. It was the perfect size for the little elf, but it looked like it would be tiny for human children hands.

Chip hiked the ball as the players from Team Toymakers raced down the field. Rhonda was able to end the play by removing one elf's scarf. After three passes, Connor came close to intercepting the chestnut. However, it was so tiny that it bounced right out of his hands.

Soon, Team Toymakers had their first touchdown.

"It's okay," said Connor in a huddle. "We just need to push through!"
But during the next play, no one on Santa's Squad was able to catch the ball.

"It's just too tiny!" said Vicky. "My hands are too big."

"We'll never be able to beat them if they can use magic to catch the ball!" said Darryl.

"And I'm sweating, making my marshmallow kneepads all sticky!" said Pete.
Connor smiled. "Sticky kneepads? Pete, you're a genius!"

"Really?" said Pete.

Connor pulled a piece of marshmallow off his knee and rubbed it on his fingers and palms. "Just one more bit of magic. I'd like to see that chestnut jump out of these hands!"

The rest of his team, except for their quarterback Jan, did the same. Their hands were stickier than glue.

Their marshmallowy fingers allowed them to catch up to Team Toymakers. After a field goal, when Don kicked the chestnut between two Christmas trees, Santa's Squad was only four points behind. Then, Team Toymakers got four downs, and Santa's Squad took possession.

But there were only ten seconds left.
Coach Claus covered his eyes with his hands.

"I can't watch, it's just too much,
My tummy feels so gross.
I'll toss my cookies if I look,
The game is just THAT close!"

Now it was Connor's turn to feel nervous. "Don't worry," said Pete. "You had a great idea, and thanks to that idea we're going to win!"

"I wouldn't have had the idea if it weren't for you!" said Connor.
"That's called teamwork!" said Pete.
They gave each other a high five… forgetting that their hands were sticky with marshmallow.
Uh oh.

The reindeer in the booth were feeling the pressure too.

"If Santa's Squad pulls this one off
Oh, what a shocking sight!"
"It will be the best comeback since
Dear Rudolph's foggy night!"

The nutcracker referee jingled the bell. Pete and Connor stepped up with their hands still stuck together.

Chip noticed and chuckled.

Jan hiked the ball and Santa's Squad rushed down the field. Team Toymaker did a very good job at covering them. There were only two open players: Connor and Pete.

As the clock wound down, Jan hurled the Chestnut down the field. It sped towards the endzone as Connor and Pete, still stuck together, ran after it.

They pumped their legs harder than they ever had in their lives. As the Chestnut began to plummet to the ground, Connor and Pete slapped their non-stuck hands together around the tiny chestnut, and their legs became firmly planted on the ground between the endzone Christmas trees.

Santa's squad erupted in cheers. They had won!

Ricky ran up to Pete and Connor. "How'd you do it?" he asked.

Pete looked at Connor and grinned. "We stuck together!"

Coach Claus was laughing so hard that his stomach bounced like a bowl full of jelly.

"We did it! We did it! We got a touch down!
The Elf Games are done!
Our team stuck together, we eked out a win,
And Santa's Squad took home the prize!"
said Coach Claus, so excited that he forgot to rhyme.

The team lifted a large jug of chocolate syrup and dumped it on Coach Claus's head. Connor and Pete used some of it to melt the marshmallows from their hands and joined the team in the celebration.

Both teams gathered in the middle of the gingerbread field as the nutcracker referee handed each member of Santa's Squad a trophy. It was a golden reindeer with a shimmering, ruby nose.

"Let this prize remind you that
You should be a good friend.
If you are, then you might get
To come back once again!"
said the referee, munching on the football.

Coach Claus gave all his players a huge hug and instructed them to press the red nose on their trophy. When Connor did, his trophy began to glow. He said goodbye to his teammates as he was whisked back home in a flash of light.

He placed his trophy above the fireplace and smiled. It was the best gift he'd ever received! His experience in the North Pole, and the friends he made, were better than any baseball!

Plus, he learned he didn't need a baseball to play baseball!

Page 19

Page 20

Page 21

Page 22

Page 23

Page 24

Page 25

Page 26

Page 27

Page 28

Page 29

Elf Games

Merry Christmas to all and to all a goodnight.

CPSIA information can be obtained
at www.ICGtesting.com
Printed in the USA
LVRC102047221121
704133LV00011B/737